It's an Armadillo!

text and photographs by

BIANCA LAVIES

A PUFFIN UNICORN

ACKNOWLEDGMENTS

for sharing time, knowledge and ideas:

Dr. Eleanor E. Storrs
Dr. Harry Burchfield
Dr. Jim Layne, Archbold Biological Station
Mr. David Austin, formerly of the Florida Game
and Freshwater Fish Commission
Mr. Dorn Whitmore, Merritt Island National Wildlife Refuge
Aletha Rector

And to Gil Grosvenor, for being an enthusiastic supporter
of my work when he was *National Geographic* magazine's editor
during my first five years on the photographic staff.

PUFFIN UNICORN BOOKS

Published by the Penguin Group
Penguin Books USA Inc., 375 Hudson Street, New York, New York 10014, U.S.A.
Penguin Books Ltd, 27 Wrights Lane, London W8 5TZ, England
Penguin Books Australia Ltd, Ringwood, Victoria, Australia
Penguin Books Canada Ltd, 10 Alcorn Avenue, Toronto, Ontario, Canada M4V 3B2
Penguin Books (N.Z.) Ltd, 182-190 Wairau Road, Auckland 10, New Zealand
Penguin Books Ltd, Registered Offices: Harmondsworth, Middlesex, England

Library of Congress number 89-31821
ISBN 0-14-050312-9

Published in the United States by Dutton Children's Books,
a division of Penguin Books USA Inc.

Designer: Riki Levinson
Printed in Hong Kong by South China Printing Co.
First Puffin Unicorn Edition 1994
10 9 8 7 6 5 4 3 2 1

IT'S AN ARMADILLO! is also available in hardcover
from Dutton Children's Books.

to Gil Grosvenor, because of his
affection for the photo on the cover
of this book

What has left these tracks in the sand?
Something with four feet and a tail.
You can see its footprints.
You can see the groove made by its tail.
Where did it go?

Into its burrow underground.
The burrow keeps it cool in summer
and warm in winter.

During the day, it sleeps there in a nest.
In the evening, it will leave the burrow.

Here it comes.
It's an armadillo!

There are several kinds of armadillos
in the world.
This one is called a nine-banded armadillo.
The bands look like stripes around
her middle.
With her nose and claws, the armadillo
roots up leaves and twigs.
She is searching for food—beetles, grubs,
and ant eggs.
Sometimes she also eats berries
or juicy roots.

Every now and then the armadillo sits up
on her hind legs and listens.
She cannot see very well, but
she can hear the sounds around her:
a leaf rustling, a twig breaking—
even a camera clicking.

She also stops to sniff the air.
Her keen sense of smell makes up for
her poor eyesight.
She can follow the trail of a cricket
just by sniffing.
Now she smells fire ants.

The armadillo starts to dig.
Her long claws make her an expert digger.
Then she sniffs the hole she has dug,
searching for ant eggs.
Ants walk along her nose.
They try to bite her, but they cannot pierce
her tough, leathery covering.
This covering is called a carapace, and
it protects her body like armor.
Armadillo is a Spanish word meaning
"little armored one."
But the armadillo does have some
soft spots—the skin on her belly,
the skin between her bands,
and the tip of her nose, for instance.

The armadillo's long, sticky tongue
flicks in and out, in and out,
lapping up the food she finds.

She has small, stubby teeth, but she doesn't use them for chewing or biting or much of anything.

Soon she ambles on, searching for more food.
She goes into dense, scrubby areas, where
her carapace lets her slip through tangles
and prickles.
Her bands allow her to bend
and turn with ease.
After a while she wanders too close
to a road.
Suddenly there is a flash of headlights.
What does the armadillo do?

She jumps!
That's what armadillos do
when they are startled.
Then they run like crazy.
This armadillo is lucky.
The car does not hit her.

She comes to a small river.
To cross it she can hold her breath, sink,
and walk along the plants on the bottom.

Or she can gulp lots of air into her stomach,
float, and paddle along like a ball with feet.
Sometimes armadillos float on logs.
People say they may have crossed
the big Mississippi River this way.
Nine-banded armadillos live in the southern
United States and all through Central and
South America.

Now the armadillo looks very fat.
Can you guess why?
Eight months ago she mated with
a male armadillo.
Soon she will have babies.
To make her nest cozy for them,
she collects grass and leaves.

She holds the grass and leaves in a bundle
between her front and hind legs.
Then she hops backwards.
As she hops, her tail guides her into the burrow.
She does this many times, until her nest
is just right.

In the nest, she gives birth to four
baby armadillos, or pups.
Each pup is exactly the same as the others.
They are identical quadruplets.
The pups nurse many times a day.

Their mother's milk helps them grow.
Armadillos are mammals.
Mammals have hair or fur, and
mammal mothers feed their young with milk
from their own bodies.

The pups are lively right from birth.
Their eyes are open, and they crawl
all over their mother, and one another.

Their mother takes good care of them.
She leaves her burrow less often now.

At first the pups' armor is soft,
smooth, and shiny.
It feels a little like wax.
The armor will become tougher
as the pups grow.
In a few months they will be big enough
and strong enough to go out on their own.
Until then they stay inside the burrow,
drink their mother's milk, and play.
They sniff one another
and crawl all over each other until...

they are all tired out.
Then they snuggle up together
and close their eyes.

They are ready for a good nap.
Sleep tight.

This armadillo may have thought Bianca Lavies was just a place to rest in a river. She was photographing the armadillo underwater when, instead of swimming to the far shore, it swam to her and climbed up on her shoulder. "After nudging its soft nose against my cheek and ear," says Bianca, "it even climbed on top of my head and started digging in my hair with its sharp claws—presumably for insects!

"When I started photographing the armadillos in this book, I knew it was not going to be easy. I knew because I had met them before, during another assignment. I was staying in a house in a swamp, and every night I was kept awake by loud banging and scraping noises underneath the floorboards. 'Armadillos,' I was told. Sometimes I saw them at dusk, but whenever I tried to sneak up on them, they would take off fast.

"The first two-and-a-half weeks I spent sneaking up on the armadillos in this book, I didn't shoot one roll of film. They were very scared of me indeed. Later I realized it was because I was in an area where armadillos had been hunted. So I traveled to two places in Florida where they are protected. It took hours of walking and lots of patience to be able to observe and photograph them."